Conscious Contact:

The Twelve Steps

As Prayer

By Dr. Mic Hunter

ISBN-13: 978-1461068969
ISBN-10: 1461068967

In an effort to place principles before personalities, members of Twelve Step-based fellowships remain anonymous at the level of press, radio, television, and other media; therefore, any name, including the author's, that appears herein is not to be taken as an indication that the named person has any affiliation with A.A. or any other Twelve Step-based fellowship.

Tags: Twelve Steps, prayer, spirituality, self-help, recovery.

Table Of Contents

The Twelve Steps Of Alcoholics Anonymous

1) We admitted we were powerless over alcohol-that our lives had become unmanageable.
2) Came to believe that a Power greater than ourselves could restore us to sanity.
3) Made a decision to turn our will and our lives over to the care of God *as we understood Him.*
4) Made a searching and fearless moral inventory of ourselves.
5) Admitted to God, to ourselves, and to another human being, the exact nature of our wrongs.
6) Were entirely ready to have God remove all these defects of character.
7) Humbly asked Him to remove our shortcomings.
8) Made a list of all persons we had harmed, and became willing to make amends to them all.
9) Made direct amends to such people wherever possible, except when to do so would injure them or others.
10) Continued to take personal inventory and when we were wrong promptly admitted it.
11) Sought through prayer and meditation to improve our conscious contact with God *as we understood Him* praying only for knowledge of God's will for us and the power to carry that out.
12) Having had a spiritual awakening as the result of these steps, we tried to carry this message to alcoholics and to practice these principles in all our affairs.

The Twelve Steps of Alcoholics Anonymous are reprinted and adapted with permission of Alcoholics Anonymous World Services, Inc. ("AAWS") Permission to adapt the Twelve Steps does not mean that AAWS has reviewed or approved the contents of this publication, or that AAWS necessarily agrees with the views expressed herein. A.A. is a program of recovery from alcoholism only - use of the Twelve Steps in connection with programs and activities which are patterned after A.A., but which address other problems, or in any other non-A.A. context, does not imply otherwise. Although Alcoholics Anonymous is a spiritual program, A.A. is not a religious program, and use of A.A. material in the present connection does not imply A.A.'s affiliation with or endorsement of, any sect, denomination, or specific religious belief.

The Twelve Steps Of Alcoholics Anonymous [Adapted]

1) We admitted we were powerless over [affliction]- that our lives had become unmanageable.

2) Came to believe that a Power greater than ourselves could restore us to sanity.

3) Made a decision to turn our will and our lives over to the care of God *as we understood* [God].

4) Made a searching and fearless moral inventory of ourselves.

5) Admitted to God, to ourselves, and to another human being, the exact nature of our wrongs.

6) Were entirely ready to have God remove all these defects of character.

7) Humbly asked [God] to remove our shortcomings.

8) Made a list of all persons we had harmed, and became willing to make amends to them all.

9) Made direct amends to such people wherever possible, except when to do so would injure them or others.

10) Continued to take personal inventory and when we were wrong promptly admitted it.

11) Sought through prayer and meditation to improve our conscious contact with God *as we understood* [God] praying only for knowledge of God's will for us and the power to carry that out.

12) Having had a spiritual awakening as the result of these steps, we tried to carry this message to [others who suffer] and to practice these principles in all our affairs.

Acknowledgements

Many thanks to Norma Hunter
and Joanna Colrain for their assistance

Introduction

For thirty years of my life I have worked with addicts. Regardless of the setting, in-patient primary treatment, outpatient mental health center, detox, hospital, or private practice, one thing has remained consistent; my belief in the power of the Twelve Step program. I know from research studies and my years of professional experience that addicts who actively practice the Steps are much more likely to remain sober and to find peace of mind than those people who go it alone. Even though I have four college degrees I find that most of what I tell my psychotherapy clients can be found in the Steps, particularly when it comes to the topic of spirituality. I guess you could say I am a Twelve Step fundamentalist; I believe everything needed for a practical spirituality is within the Steps. I sincerely hope that the prayers that follow will inspire, guide, and comfort you.

Mic Hunter

A Spiritual Program Means Spiritual Problems Will Likely Arise

"He listens equally to the prayers of the believer and the unbeliever."

Henry David Thoreau, American poet

It doesn't take long before one is faced with the spiritual aspects of the Twelve Step program-there it is already in the Second Step. As it says in *Alcoholics Anonymous*, (a.k.a. the Big Book), "We were squarely confronted with the question of faith. We couldn't duck the issue."[1] Clearly the Twelve Step program has a spiritual basis. Seven of the Steps directly reference spirituality in some form.

Both newcomers and old-timers report that admitting powerlessness and unmanageability (Step One) is easier for them than conceding there is a power greater than themselves (Step Two). The inability to make such an acknowledgment is a common roadblock to working the remaining Steps and obtaining a serene recovery. The blocks are many: unpleasant previous experiences with religion; confusing one's parental relationship with one's relationship with God; a belief in the need to be independent; and, a history of abuse or neglect which lead to wondering, "Where was God when all that was happening to me?"

The early members of Alcoholics Anonymous found that spirituality was such a vital part of their recovery that every edition of the Big Book has contained a chapter, "We Agnostics," which advises readers that their affliction is, "an illness which only a spiritual experience will conquer."[2] In addition readers are warned, "We are not cured of [affliction]. What we really have is a daily reprieve contingent on the maintenance of our spiritual condition."[3] If you are struggling with whether or not to practice a spiritual program, I suggest you read the entire chapter, "We Agnostics", as well as the material on Steps Two and Three in *Twelve Steps And Twelve Traditions,* and *The Twelve Steps & Shame,* as well as some of the many published resources on the topic.[4] Ask your sponsor and others at meetings how they overcame their resistance to spirituality, and how spirituality has been helpful to them in their recovery. Your happiness, if not your life, depends on learning these lessons.

"To pray is to think about the meaning of life."

Ludwig Wittgenstein

The Importance Of Ritual

"**ritual.** An oft-repeated pattern of behavior which tends to occur at appropriate times."

Dictionary Of Psychology. [5]

According to philosopher Thomas Moore meaningful spirituality requires, "...attention, mindfulness, regularity, and devotion. It asks for some small measure of withdrawal from a world set up to ignore soul."[6] Taking part in ritual is one method for obtaining this temporary withdrawal. Engaging in a ritual at the beginning of an event indicates something important is about to take place, and helps participants clear their minds of distractions in order focus their attention in the present moment. A ritual at the end of an event signals to all concerned that the experience is over and it is appropriate to go on with daily living.

Although rituals are commonly used in settings such as sporting events (singing the national anthem) and educational settings (wearing a gown and mortar board with a tassel), when it comes to spiritual rituals some people get intimidated. They think spiritual rituals require elaborate or mysterious rites, and so shy away from utilizing rituals as a part of their spiritual practice. This misunderstanding is unfortunate since the use of rituals can greatly enhance one's practice of spirituality. Thomas Moore suggested, "Spirituality need not be grandiose in its ceremonials. Indeed, the soul might benefit most when its spiritual life is performed in the context it favors-ordinary daily vernacular life."[7]

Besides the belief that for a ritual to be effective it must be grand and extraordinary, another block to the effective use of ritual is the idea that rituals are to be taken literally. Rituals are meant to be symbolic. Moore offered this explanation, "Ritual is an action that speaks to the mind and the heart but doesn't necessarily make sense in a literal context. In church people do not eat bread in order to feed their bodies but to nourish their souls."[8]

Anyone who has traveled to different cities and attended Twelve Step meetings will tell you that the rituals used to begin and end meetings vary from group to group. The Fourth Tradition protects this variety, "Each group should be autonomous except in matters affecting other groups or [the fellowship] as a whole."[9] One group begins with a moment of silence for those who still suffer, while across town another group passes around, "How It Works," so each member gets a chance to read a paragraph. When it comes to ending a meeting the rituals also vary from group to group. These rituals help make a Twelve Step meeting more than merely a gathering of people casually talking.

Just as rituals help group members get more out of meetings, personal rituals prior to prayer assist individuals in obtaining more from the experience of prayer. Common examples of such a ritual are a Roman Catholic making the sign of the cross before and after saying a prayer, or a Muslim unrolling a prayer rug on which to kneel. You may wish to utilize rituals from your spiritual or religious background into your prayer activities. If you don't already have such rituals then I suggest you create your own. For example, lighting a candle, which is burned only during prayer. What matters is, not so much the specific actions, but more that they are done with intention. The word *intention* comes from the Latin roots *in* and *tendere* that mean, "to stretch the mind into."[10] In other words, if you intend an action to be a ritual, it is a ritual.

Those that balk at the idea of taking part in rituals as a part of recovery fail to realize that they have long been involved in rituals related to their affliction. For example, the sex addict who engages in a long ritual of trying on an assortment of underwear and outfits prior to going out to find a sex partner; the time spent on putting on and taking off the various articles of clothing is part of the high, without it she doesn't get the same buzz. Another example is the drug addict who savors the tasks involved in preparing to ingest the intoxicating substance, whether it is alcohol or some other drug. Ritual is so powerful that some people report the ritual of tying off their arms with a rubber hose and penetrating their skin with a hypodermic needle gives them a sense of well-being, even when no drug is actually injected

The Hazard Of Ritualism

"ritualism, *n.* A religious or semi-religious ceremony fixed by law, precept, or custom, with the essential oil of sincerity carefully squeezed out of it."

Ambrose Bierce, The Devil's Dictionary, 1881

Even though ritual is a powerful tool it can lose its effectiveness. If the person who is engaging in the ritual does so mindlessly, merely going through the motions of the ritual while thinking about something else, then the ritual become meaningless. This can happen in Twelve Step meetings. The participants merely mouth the words of the serenity prayer or think about what's for dinner, while "How It Works" is read.

Some people are taught that rituals are only useful, *ex opere operato*, meaning "from the thing done."[11] This belief holds that it is the ritual itself that makes the experience powerful. Therefore, they focus primarily on doing the ritual correctly.

Unfortunately, excessive focus on doing it right can soon lead to the ritual becoming robotic once it is memorized and can be done thoughtlessly. If the person performing the prescribed acts doesn't have the proper intent, the actions lose their meaning. In other words, without an attitude of reverence the ritual loses it power, even if the behaviors are performed perfectly according to tradition. The American psychologist Erich Fromm was warning of the hazards of ritualism when he said, "What at one time was a dynamic structure, mediating between man and his destiny and interpersonal responsibilities, has become mere mechanical ritual that dwarfs man rather than strengthening them." When Jesus of Nazareth preached, "The Sabbath was made for people and not people for the Sabbath," fellow Jews were shocked at his words.[12] With this single statement he was instructing his followers that whenever they were engaging in any tradition rather than blindly engaging in the behavior with no understanding of its purpose they ought to think about, be guided by, and act according to, the original intent of the tradition, The story of the farmer who was plowing his field on the Sabbath also illustrates this concept. According to this story there was a clergyman from a farmer's church who passed by the farm on his way home from Sabbath services. When he saw the farmer in the field plowing the clergyman exclaimed, "I noticed you weren't in church today." The farmer stopped plowing and replied, "Yeah, well, I figured God would rather have me sitting on my plow thinking about spiritual matters, than to have me sitting in church but thinking about all the plowing I had to get to." This farmer was a person who was more interested in the spirit of the Sabbath than the traditional expression of it.

Unfortunately many people haven't yet learned this lesson. When I was a young man I became romantically involved with a woman who was raised in the Roman Catholic tradition. Her parents insisted if I was seriously considering marrying their daughter I would have to convert to her religion. When I attended my first mass I watched as the members of the congregation kneeled, crossed themselves, genuflected, and engaged in all sorts of rituals that were totally unfamiliar to me. I was naturally curious about what was expected of me, as well as the meaning of the various actions. I kept asking, "What is the symbolism of that?" Much to my surprise none of my in-laws-to-be could explain the reasons they were doing what they were doing. The best explanation they could give me was, "That just the way it's done." They assured me that after a few weeks I would have memorized what to do and then I, "wouldn't have to think about it anymore." Given their attitude it appeared to me they viewed the ritual of mass as merely an obligation, something done to avoid going to hell, but not something meaningful and empowering.

For far too many people prayer is an act that has become so ritualized it has become nearly devoid of meaning for them. If one merely repeats the words of a prayer without thinking about the meaning of them, then it becomes boring and insignificant.

Edgar Jackson, psychologist and minister described the problem this way:

> Sometimes the institution that should know most about prayer misdirects those who turn to it for guidance. The church often leaves its people with the impression that prayer is primarily a matter of pious word formations... How much more difficult it is to learn the language of the spirit, where feelings are more important than words, and aspirations more significant than syntax.[13] The teaching of rote prayers often anesthetizes our spiritual sensitivities. The capacity of awe and wonder so essential to effective prayer is often stunted in children who are drilled in the form and formality rather than in the feeling of genuine prayer. Growth in spiritual communication is enriched by that culture where creative and individualistic expression is permitted.[14]

Any form of prayer can become ritualized, the shortcoming lies, not in the prayer, but in the person praying. In order for prayer to be meaningful one must be mentally and emotionally present while taking part in it. When I was young my father used to say a prayer prior to beginning the evening meal. He did this because his mother had done it when he was a child, and she told him it would be a good idea to continue the tradition when he had children. Unfortunately, my father spoke the prayer so rapidly that neither my brother nor myself could understand what he was saying; in fact we both thought he was speaking in some language other than English. It was only years later when we were at our grandmother's house and she began the meal with a prayer that we realized that, for all these years both she and our father had been saying the same words. The difference was that our grandmother spoke them in a slow deliberate manner and was understandable.

"Without reverence, rituals are empty."

Paul Woodruff, professor of humanities[15]

Suggestions For Using The Provided Prayers

"**prayer,** humble entreaty addressed to God; any set formula for praying to God; any spiritual communion with God."

Webster's Dictionary

In an effort to avoid prayer becoming stale I have provided several different interpretations of the Twelve Steps to be used as prayer. These various versions can be utilized independently or combined with other forms of prayer. The purpose is to provide you with a Twelve Step-based foundation that you can modify to suit your form of spirituality. In order to fully experience what a version has to offer you may want to stick to one version until you are comfortable doing it before moving on to another version. Regardless of which version you decide to use, I suggest that you make an attempt to pray at approximately the same time each morning and evening.

Most people find it easiest to pray first thing in the morning and right before going to bed. In addition, speaking aloud during prayer can be very powerful as it helps people to be more present in the moment. With practice you may find that the amount of time you spend in prayer will increase, as well as experiencing an increase in quality of your prayer. Such improvements are the result of having a structure.

Finally, you may wish to engage in prayer where you and at least one other person pray aloud together. If you have previously attended a Twelve Step meeting, then it is likely you have already experienced praying as part of a group. In addition to praying as a part of the ritual of a meeting, I'm suggesting you take things a bit farther and invite one or more people who are important to you to pray together. This can be a highly intimate act. Whatever you decide to do, experiment, practice, and trust yourself.

No form of prayer is useful if you don't practice it on a regular basis. In all my years of working with addicts and other afflictions I have never found an addict who thought it was too cold, too late, he was too tired or too busy to engage in addictive behavior, but I have met plenty of people who had plenty of excuses to avoid recovery behaviors. In the past you found the time to engage in the behaviors associated with your affliction on a frequent, if not daily, basis. I hope you will now make time to practice your recovery behaviors each day.

Before reading the prayers I have formulated, read this portion of a prayer based on the seventh Step by Larry E. a member of Sex Addicts Anonymous.

"I know a little:
That I am powerless over my addiction;
That I cannot remove my shortcomings alone but do my part;
That I must humbly ask for help;
That I must surrender the result;
That I must be grateful;
That I am now ready to have You remove all my shortcomings."[16]

As you can see Larry created this prayer starting with language from the first Step (powerlessness), went on using terms from Step seven, (shortcomings, humbly), and then added the concept of gratitude. I include this prayer, not only because I like it, but also in order to stress that anyone can utilize the concepts and terms found in the Steps to formulate their own prayers.

Version One
Keep It Simple

"The fewer the words, the better the prayer."

Version one is a straightforward use of the Twelve Steps that is personalized by the use of the singular (*I*) rather than the plural (*we*) that is usually used in the Steps. In addition the tense of the wording is changed from the past tense into the present tense. For example in Step One "admitted" is changed to "admit." Finally, the phrase "when isolated" is added as a reminder that recovery is best accomplished with the support of others. Alone an individual is likely to remain powerless to stop the behaviors that result in harm to self, family members, and the society in general. The Steps refer to all this destruction simply as *unmanageability*.

There are two forms of the prayer presented; one for beginning the day, and one for ending the day. The morning version makes use of seven of the Steps (1, 2, 3, 6, 7, 11, & 12). The evening version makes use of the same seven Steps, but also includes use of three additional Steps (8, 9, & 10).

The morning version is used to help make a conscious commitment to recovery for each new day. Beginning the day in this way helps keep the focus on practicing the Steps as one goes about the tasks of daily living. The evening version is designed to help in reflection and acknowledgment, as well as increasing gratitude and in measuring progress.

Version One-Morning

(Engage in your beginning ritual if you are using one.)

THIS MORNING I ADMIT WHEN ISOLATED I
AM POWERLESS OVER (Fill in problem)-WHICH
MAKES MY LIFE UNMANAGEABLE.

THIS MORNING I BELIEVE THERE IS A POWER
GREATER THAN MYSELF THAT CAN RESTORE
ME TO SANITY.

THIS MORNING I AM MAKING A DECISION
TO TURN MY WILL AND MY LIFE OVER TO MY
HIGHER POWER'S CARE.

THIS MORNING I AM ENTIRELY READY TO
HAVE MY HIGHER POWER REMOVE ALL MY
DEFECTS OF CHARACTER.

THIS MORNING I'M HUMBLY ASKING
MY HIGHER POWER TO REMOVE MY
SHORTCOMINGS.

THIS MORNING I AM SEEKING THROUGH
PRAYER AND MEDITATION TO IMPROVE MY
CONSCIOUS CONTACT WITH MY HIGHER
POWER; I AM PRAYING ONLY FOR KNOWLEDGE
OF MY HIGHER POWER'S WILL FOR ME, AND
THE POWER TO CARRY THAT OUT.

TODAY AS I EXPERIENCE A SPIRITUAL
AWAKENING AS A RESULT OF THESE STEPS,
I WILL TRY TO CARRY THIS MESSAGE TO
OTHERS WHO STILL SUFFER AND TO PRACTICE
THESE PRINCIPLES IN ALL ASPECTS OF MY LIFE.

(Engage in your ending ritual if you are using one.)

Version One-Evening

(Engage in your beginning ritual if you are using one.)

TONIGHT I ADMIT WHEN ISOLATED I AM
POWERLESS OVER (Fill in problem)-THAT MY
LIFE IS UNMANAGEABLE.

TONIGHT I BELIEVE THERE IS A POWER
GREATER THAN MYSELF THAT IS RESTORING
ME TO SANITY.

TONIGHT I AM GRATEFUL THAT THIS DAY I
WAS ABLE TO MAKE A DECISION TO TURN
MY WILL AND MY LIFE OVER TO MY HIGHER
POWER'S CARE.

TONIGHT I CONTINUE TO BE ENTIRELY
WILLING TO HAVE MY HIGHER POWER
REMOVE ALL MY DEFECTS OF CHARACTER.

TONIGHT I HUMBLY ASK MY HIGHER
POWER TO CONTINUE TO REMOVE MY
SHORTCOMINGS.

TONIGHT AS I TAKE PERSONAL INVENTORY
I FIND I HAVE BEEN WRONG AND NOW
PROMPTLY ADMIT IT. (If after an honest review
of the day you are unable to identify anyone you
have harmed, replace the above with "TONIGHT
AS I TAKE PERSONAL INVENTORY I FIND THAT
I HAVEN'T WRONGED ANYONE," skip the next
two sentences.)

TONIGHT I LIST THESE PERSONS I HAVE
HARMED TODAY, AND AM WILLING TO MAKE
AMENDS TO THEM ALL.

TONIGHT I AGREE TO MAKE DIRECT AMENDS
TO THESE PEOPLE WHEREVER POSSIBLE,
EXCEPT WHEN TO DO SO WOULD INJURE
THEM OR OTHERS.

TONIGHT I AGAIN SEEK THROUGH
PRAYER AND MEDITATION TO IMPROVE MY
CONSCIOUS CONTACT WITH MY HIGHER
POWER. I AM PRAYING ONLY FOR KNOWLEDGE
OF MY HIGHER POWER'S WILL FOR ME, AND
THE POWER TO CARRY THAT OUT.

TODAY I AM GRATEFUL I EXPERIENCED A
SPIRITUAL AWAKENING AS A RESULT OF
THESE STEPS. I AM PROUD THAT I TRIED
TO CARRY THIS MESSAGE TO OTHERS WHO
STILL SUFFER AND THAT I PRACTICED
THESE PRINCIPLES IN ALL ASPECTS OF MY
LIFE.

Conscious Contact

Version Two
Breathe!

You will notice this version is similar to version one; however in this version you are encouraged to pause between each statement to more fully appreciate their importance. The word *spirit* comes from the Latin word *spirare*, which means, "to breathe." Therefore, you can think of each breath as a spiritual act. I recommend taking at least one full breath, in and out, between each sentence. Use this time to focus your attention on the meaning of the phrase you have just spoken, and on how it applies to your life this day.

Version Two- Morning

(Engage in your beginning ritual if you are using one.)

THIS MORNING I ADMIT WHEN ISOLATED
I AM POWERLESS OVER <u>(Fill in problem)</u>.
(BREATHE)

THIS MORNING I ADMIT WHEN I RELY ONLY
ON MY WILL MY LIFE IS UNMANAGEABLE.
(BREATHE)

THIS MORNING I BELIEVE THERE IS A POWER
GREATER THAN MYSELF. (BREATHE)

THIS MORNING I BELIEVE THIS POWER
CAN, AND WILL, RESTORE ME TO SANITY.
(BREATHE)

THIS MORNING I AM MAKING A DECISION TO
TURN MY WILL OVER TO THAT POWER'S CARE.
(BREATHE)

THIS MORNING I AM MAKING A DECISION TO
TURN MY LIFE OVER TO THAT POWER'S CARE.
(BREATHE)

THIS MORNING I AM ENTIRELY READY TO
HAVE THAT POWER REMOVE ALL MY DEFECTS
OF CHARACTER. (BREATHE)

THIS MORNING I HUMBLY ASK THAT POWER
TO REMOVE MY SHORTCOMINGS. (BREATHE)

THIS MORNING I AM SEEKING THROUGH
THIS PRAYER TO IMPROVE MY CONSCIOUS
CONTACT WITH THAT SPIRITUAL POWER.
(BREATHE)

THIS MORNING I AM PRAYING FOR KNOWLEDGE OF THAT SPIRITUAL POWER'S WILL FOR ME. (BREATHE)

THIS MORNING I AM PRAYING FOR THE POWER TO CARRY OUT THAT SPIRITUAL POWER'S WILL FOR ME. (BREATHE)

THIS MORNING I AM PRAYING FOR THE WILLINGNESS TO TAKE THE ACTION NECESSARY TO CARRY OUT THAT SPIRITUAL POWER'S WILL FOR ME. (BREATHE)

THIS MORNING I AM PRAYING FOR A SPIRITUAL AWAKENING. (BREATHE)

THIS MORNING I AM PRAYING FOR THE OPPORTUNITY TO CARRY THIS MESSAGE TO OTHERS WHO STILL SUFFER. (BREATHE)

THIS MORNING I AM PRAYING FOR THE ABILITY AND WILLINGNESS TO PRACTICE THESE PRINCIPLES IN ALL ASPECTS OF MY LIFE.

(Engage in your ending ritual if you are using one.)

Version Two- Evening

(Engage in your beginning ritual if you are using one.)

TONIGHT I ADMIT IN ISOLATION I AM
POWERLESS OVER (Fill in problem)-THAT MY
LIFE IS UNMANAGEABLE.
 (BREATHE)

TONIGHT I BELIEVE THAT YOU ARE A POWER
GREATER THAN MYSELF AND YOU ARE
RESTORING ME TO SANITY. (BREATHE)

TONIGHT I AM GRATEFUL THIS DAY I WAS
ABLE TO MAKE A DECISION TO TURN MY
WILL AND MY LIFE OVER TO YOUR CARE.
(BREATHE)

TONIGHT I CONTINUE TO BE ENTIRELY
WILLING TO HAVE YOU REMOVE ALL MY
DEFECTS OF CHARACTER. (BREATHE)

TONIGHT I HUMBLY ASK YOU TO CONTINUE
TO REMOVE MY SHORTCOMINGS. (BREATHE)

TONIGHT I TAKE PERSONAL INVENTORY
AND FIND I HAVE BEEN WRONG AND NOW
PROMPTLY ADMIT IT TO YOU. (If after an honest review of the day you are unable to identify
anyone you have harmed, skip the next two sentences.) (BREATHE)

TONIGHT I LIST THESE PERSONS I HAVE
HARMED TODAY, AND AM WILLING TO MAKE
AMENDS TO THEM ALL. (BREATHE)

TONIGHT I AGREE TO MAKE DIRECT AMENDS
TO THESE PEOPLE WHEREVER POSSIBLE,
EXCEPT WHEN TO DO SO WOULD INJURE
THEM OR OTHERS. (BREATHE)

TONIGHT I AM SEEKING THROUGH PRAYER TO
IMPROVE MY CONSCIOUS CONTACT WITH YOU.
(BREATHE)

TONIGHT I AM PRAYING FOR KNOWLEDGE OF
YOUR WILL FOR ME. (BREATHE)

TONIGHT I AM PRAYING FOR THE <u>POWER</u> TO
CARRY OUT YOUR WILL FOR ME. (BREATHE)

TONIGHT I AM PRAYING FOR THE
<u>WILLINGNESS</u> TO CARRY OUT YOUR WILL
FOR ME. (BREATHE)

TONIGHT I AM SEEKING THROUGH
MEDITATION TO IMPROVE MY CONSCIOUS
CONTACT WITH YOU. (BREATHE)

TODAY I EXPERIENCED A SPIRITUAL
AWAKENING AS A RESULT OF THESE STEPS.
(BREATHE)

TODAY I TRIED TO CARRY THIS MESSAGE TO
OTHERS WHO STILL SUFFER. (BREATHE)

TODAY I PRACTICED THESE PRINCIPLES IN
ALL MY AFFAIRS.

(Engage in your beginning ritual if you are using one.)

Version Three-
The Essentials Of Recovery

"You pray in your distress and in your need;
would that you might pray also in the fullness
of your joy and in your days of abundance. "

Kahlil Gibran, Lebanese poet (1883-1931)

In this next version Steps One through Three are combined with a portion of, "How It Works," which many A.A. meetings (and other fellowships) use as a portion of their opening.[17] Utilizing this passage is useful in that it provides an overlap between your personal spiritual practices of prayer and meditation with the public practice of attending meetings. Eventually each time you are in a meeting and hear, "How It Works," you will be reminded of how your Higher Power works through your relationships with other people and when you pray by yourself it will remind you of your personal relationship with your Higher Power.

Prayer can be conceptualized as speaking to your Higher Power, and meditation as listening to your Higher Power. Many persons short-change themselves when it comes to a relationship with their Higher Power. They have a one-way relationship. They talk to their Higher Power, but do not listen. Imagine how little you would learn if you never listened but only spoke in meetings! The same is true of your relationship with your Higher Power.

Version three contains some of the words from the section titled, "Spiritual Experience," in the Big Book.[18] Version three has an increased emphasis on meditation. Most spiritual traditions have meditation as an important tool in forming and maintaining a meaningful relationship with their concept of a Higher Power. In version three you are asked to take time to be silent and to listen for your Higher Power's will for you.

"The value of persistent prayer is not that He will hear us, but that we will finally hear Him."

William McGill

God, Is That You?

Dr. Carl Jung (whose writing influenced Bill W.) warned that, "The inner voice is at once our greatest danger and an indispensable help." When meditating, how does one know if what comes into awareness is the will of one's Higher Power, or merely the result of the insane thinking mentioned in Step Two? The process of determining what is God's will and what is one's own will is called discernment. There are various methods of discernment. Comedian Woody Allen's method is unambiguous, "If only God would give me a some clear sign! Like making a large deposit in my name in a Swiss bank account." Short of large deposits or other materials indications, what other methods of discernment have proven useful? The method I recommend consists of asking six questions concerning what came into awareness during meditation:

Is the focus on my behavior?

Is it simple?

Is it something I can do now or soon?

Does it align with my principles?

Would I be comfortable telling others?

Do I have a sense of peace when I think about it?

Is The Focus On My Behavior?

The Eleventh Step suggests praying for knowledge of God's will for oneself, not for ideas on how other people ought to behave.

Is It Simple?

The motto, "Keep it simple," serves as a reminder to avoid unnecessary complexity. An idea that involves complex plans and a cast of thousands is less likely to be the will of God than a straightforward do-the-next-right-thing action.

Is It Something I Can Do Now Or Soon?

The motto, "One day at a time," is encouragement to focus on the here and now. Regardless of what is planned for the future, action can only take place in the present. If what came into awareness during meditation can be done presently then it is more likely to be God's will than if it focused on actions in the distant future.

Does It Align With My Principles?

Over the years people have asked, "What exactly are the principles mentioned in Step twelve that we are supposed to be practicing?" One answer is, "The opposite of one's character defects referenced in Step six." But that remedy isn't very specific, so various people have listed the principles found within the Steps including:
Being hopeful
Being willing
Being humble
Being of service to others.

If a potential behavior corresponds to these principles, then it has the characteristics of what most people believe is God's will.

Would I Be Comfortable Telling Others?

Any time someone finds herself thinking, "I'm sure what came to me during meditation was my

Higher Power's will for me, but other people wouldn't understand, so I'll keep it to myself," she is treading in dangerous territory. Anything that has to be kept secret ought to be suspect; if one can imagine being comfortable telling one's sponsor or talking in a meeting about an action, then it passes the test.

Do I Have A Sense Of Peace?

If one has a sense of peace when thinking about a potential action, even though it may involve difficulties and challenges, then that is an indication that it is God's will.

Version Three- Morning

(Start with your beginning ritual)

THIS MORNING THREE PERTINENT IDEAS ARE CLEAR TO ME:

(A) I AM _____ (Your affliction, e.g. alcoholic) AND WHEN ISOLATED CANNOT MANAGE MY OWN LIFE. (BREATHE)

(B) THAT PROBABLY NO HUMAN POWER CAN RELIEVE MY AFFLICTION. (BREATHE)

(C) THAT GOD (Or other name) CAN AND WILL RELIEVE MY AFFLICTION IF SOUGHT. (BREATHE)

I AM NOW SEEKING THAT GOD (Or other name). (BREATHE)

THIS MORNING I AM ENTIRELY READY TO HAVE GOD (Or other name) REMOVE ALL MY DEFECTS OF CHARACTER. (BREATHE)

THIS MORNING I HUMBLY ASK GOD (Or other name) TO REMOVE MY SHORTCOMINGS. (BREATHE)

THIS MORNING I AM SEEKING THROUGH
THIS PRAYER TO IMPROVE MY CONSCIOUS
CONTACT WITH GOD (Or other name). I
PRAY FOR THE ESSENTIALS OF RECOVERY,
WILLINGNESS, HONESTY, AND OPEN
MINDEDNESS. (BREATHE)

THIS MORNING I AM PRAYING FOR KNOWLEDGE
OF GOD'S (Or other name) WILL FOR ME.
(BREATHE)

THIS MORNING I AM PRAYING FOR THE
POWER TO CARRY OUT GOD'S (Or other name)
WILL FOR ME. (BREATHE)

THIS MORNING I AM PRAYING FOR THE
WILLINGNESS TO TAKE THE ACTION
NECESSARY TO CARRY OUT GOD'S (Or other
name) WILL FOR ME. (BREATHE)

THIS MORNING I AM PRAYING FOR A
SPIRITUAL AWAKENING AS A RESULT OF
THESE STEPS. (BREATHE)

THIS MORNING I AM PRAYING FOR THE
OPPORTUNITY TO CARRY THIS MESSAGE TO
OTHERS WHO STILL SUFFER. (BREATHE)

THIS MORNING I AM PRAYING FOR THE
ABILITY AND WILLINGNESS TO PRACTICE
THESE PRINCIPLES IN ALL ASPECTS OF MY
LIFE. (BREATHE)

THIS MORNING I AM SEEKING THROUGH
MEDITATION TO IMPROVE MY CONSCIOUS
CONTACT WITH GOD (Or other name).
Continue to breathe for several cycles or longer,
and listen for what comes to you in the silence.
once you have a sense of your Higher Power's will
for you, state it in a simple sentence that you can
remember and reflect on throughout the day.

(Finish with your ending ritual.)

Version Three- Evening

(Start with your beginning ritual.)

THIS EVENING THREE PERTINENT IDEAS ARE
CLEAR TO ME:

(A) I AM _____ (Your affliction) AND
IN ISOLATION FROM OTHERS I CANNOT
MANAGE MY OWN LIFE. (BREATHE)

(B) THAT PROBABLY NO HUMAN POWER CAN
RELIEVE MY AFFLICTION. (BREATHE)

(C) THAT MY HIGHER POWER CAN, AND DID,
RELIEVE MY AFFLICTION TODAY. (BREATHE)

TONIGHT I CONTINUE TO BE ENTIRELY
WILLING TO HAVE MY HIGHER POWER
REMOVE ALL MY DEFECTS OF CHARACTER.
(BREATHE)

TONIGHT I HUMBLY ASK MY HIGHER
POWER TO CONTINUE TO REMOVE MY
SHORTCOMINGS EVEN AS I SLEEP. (BREATHE)

TONIGHT I TAKE PERSONAL INVENTORY
AND FIND I HAVE BEEN WRONG AND NOW
PROMPTLY ADMIT IT TO MY HIGHER POWER.
(If after an honest review of the day you are unable
to identify anyone you have harmed, replace the

statement above with "tonight after taking personal inventory I find that I have not harmed anyone," skip the next two sentences.) (BREATHE)

TONIGHT I LIST THESE PERSONS I HAVE HARMED TODAY, AND AM WILLING TO MAKE AMENDS TO THEM ALL. (BREATHE)

TONIGHT I AGREE TO MAKE DIRECT AMENDS TO THESE PEOPLE WHEREVER POSSIBLE, EXCEPT WHEN TO DO SO WOULD INJURE THEM OR OTHERS. (BREATHE)

TONIGHT I AM SEEKING THROUGH PRAYER TO IMPROVE MY CONSCIOUS CONTACT WITH MY HIGHER POWER. (BREATHE)

TONIGHT I AM PRAYING FOR KNOWLEDGE OF MY HIGHER POWER'S WILL FOR ME. (BREATHE)

TONIGHT I AM PRAYING FOR THE POWER TO CARRY OUT MY HIGHER POWER'S WILL FOR ME. (BREATHE)

TONIGHT I AM AWARE OF MY DESIRE TO CARRY OUT MY HIGHER POWER'S WILL FOR ME. (BREATHE)

TONIGHT I AM GRATEFUL TO REFLECT ON HOW TODAY I HAVE EXPERIENCED A SPIRITUAL AWAKENING AS A RESULT OF THE TWELVE STEPS. (BREATHE)

TONIGHT I AM GRATEFUL TO RECALL HOW TODAY I WAS ABLE TO CARRY THE MESSAGE OF RECOVERY TO OTHERS WHO STILL SUFFER. (BREATHE)

TONIGHT I GRATEFUL TO RECALL HOW I WAS ABLE TO PRACTICE THE PRINCIPLES OF THE TWELVE STEPS IN ALL ASPECTS OF MY LIFE. (BREATHE)

TONIGHT I AM SEEKING THROUGH MEDITATION TO IMPROVE MY CONSCIOUS CONTACT WITH MY HIGHER POWER. Continue to breathe for several cycles, and listen for what comes to you in the silence. (BREATHE)

(Finish with your ending ritual.)

Version Four
Prayer Within Prayer

Version four incorporates the Third Step and Seventh Step prayers found in *Alcoholics Anonymous,* better known as, "The Big Book."[19]

Version Four- Morning

(Start with your beginning ritual.)

THIS MORNING I ADMIT WHEN ISOLATED I AM POWERLESS OVER (Affliction). (BREATHE)

THIS MORNING I ADMIT MY LIFE IS UNMANAGEABLE WHEN I ATTEMPT TO RUN IT BY MY WILL ALONE. (BREATHE)

THIS MORNING I BELIEVE YOU EXIST. (BREATHE)

THIS MORNING I BELIEVE YOU ARE A POWER GREATER THAN MYSELF. (BREATHE)

THIS MORNING I BELIEVE YOU CAN RESTORE ME TO SANITY. (BREATHE)

THIS MORNING I OFFER MYSELF TO YOU-TO BUILD WITH ME AND DO WITH ME AS YOU WILL. (BREATHE)

THIS MORNING I PRAY THAT YOU RELIEVE ME OF THE BONDAGE OF SELF, THAT I MAY BETTER DO YOUR WILL. (BREATHE)

I PRAY YOU TAKE AWAY MY DIFFICULTIES, THAT VICTORY OVER THEM MAY BEAR WITNESS TO THOSE I WOULD HELP. (BREATHE)

THIS MORNING I AM ENTIRELY READY TO HAVE YOU REMOVE ALL MY DEFECTS OF CHARACTER. (BREATHE)

THIS MORNING I AM NOW WILLING THAT YOU SHOULD HAVE ALL OF ME- GOOD AND BAD. (BREATHE)

I PRAY THAT YOU NOW REMOVE FROM ME EVERY SINGLE DEFECT OF CHARACTER WHICH STANDS IN THE WAY OF MY USEFULNESS TO YOU AND MY FELLOWS. (BREATHE)

GRANT ME STRENGTH, AS I GO OUT FROM
HERE TO DO YOUR BIDDING. (BREATHE)

THIS MORNING I AM SEEKING THROUGH
THIS PRAYER TO IMPROVE MY CONSCIOUS
CONTACT WITH YOU. (BREATHE)

THIS MORNING I AM PRAYING FOR
KNOWLEDGE OF YOUR WILL FOR ME.
(BREATHE)

THIS MORNING I AM PRAYING FOR THE
POWER TO CARRY OUT YOUR WILL FOR ME.
(BREATHE)

THIS MORNING I AM PRAYING FOR THE
WILLINGNESS TO TAKE THE ACTION NECESSARY
TO CARRY OUT YOUR WILL FOR ME. (BREATHE)

THIS MORNING I AM PRAYING FOR A
SPIRITUAL AWAKENING AS A RESULT OF
THESE STEPS. (BREATHE)

THIS MORNING I AM PRAYING FOR THE
OPPORTUNITY TO CARRY THIS MESSAGE TO
OTHERS WHO STILL SUFFER. (BREATHE)

THIS MORNING I AM PRAYING FOR THE
ABILITY AND WILLINGNESS TO PRACTICE
THESE PRINCIPLES IN ALL ASPECTS OF MY
LIFE.

(Finish with your ending ritual.)

Version Four- Evening

(Start with your beginning ritual.)

THIS EVENING I ADMIT WHEN ISOLATED
FROM OTHERS I AM POWERLESS OVER
(Affliction). (BREATHE)

THIS EVENING I ADMIT MY LIFE IS
UNMANAGEABLE WHEN I ATTEMPT TO RUN
IT BY MY WILL ALONE. (BREATHE)

THIS EVENING I BELIEVE YOU EXIST.
(BREATHE)

THIS EVENING I BELIEVE YOU ARE A POWER
GREATER THAN MYSELF. (BREATHE)

THIS EVENING I BELIEVE THIS DAY YOU
RESTORED ME TO SANITY. (BREATHE)

THIS EVENING I CONTINUE TO OFFER
MYSELF TO YOU-TO BUILD WITH ME AND DO
WITH ME AS YOU WILL. (BREATHE)

THIS EVENING I PRAY THAT YOU CONTINUE
TO RELIEVE ME OF THE BONDAGE OF
SELF, THAT I MAY BETTER DO YOUR WILL.
(BREATHE)

THIS EVENING I PRAY YOU TAKE AWAY MY DIFFICULTIES, THAT VICTORY OVER THEM MAY BEAR WITNESS TO THOSE I WOULD HELP. (BREATHE)

THIS EVENING I CONTINUE TO BE ENTIRELY READY TO HAVE YOU REMOVE ALL MY DEFECTS OF CHARACTER. (BREATHE)

THIS EVENING I CONTINUE TO BE WILLING THAT YOU SHOULD HAVE ALL OF ME, GOOD AND BAD. (BREATHE)

THIS EVENING I PRAY THAT YOU CONTINUE TO REMOVE FROM ME EVERY SINGLE DEFECT OF CHARACTER WHICH STANDS IN THE WAY OF MY USEFULNESS TO YOU AND MY FELLOWS. (BREATHE)

I AM GRATEFUL THAT THIS DAY YOU GRANTED ME STRENGTH, AS I WENT OUT AND DID YOUR BIDDING. (BREATHE)

THIS EVENING I AM SEEKING THROUGH THIS PRAYER TO IMPROVE MY CONSCIOUS CONTACT WITH YOU. (BREATHE)

THIS EVENING I AM PRAYING FOR KNOWLEDGE OF YOUR WILL FOR ME. (BREATHE)

THIS EVENING I AM PRAYING FOR THE
POWER TO CARRY OUT YOUR WILL FOR ME.
(BREATHE)

THIS EVENING I AM PRAYING FOR THE
WILLINGNESS TO TAKE THE ACTION
NECESSARY TO CARRY OUT YOUR WILL FOR
ME. (BREATHE)

THIS EVENING I OFFER A PRAYER OF
THANKS FOR THE SPIRITUAL AWAKENING I
EXPERIENCED TODAY AS A RESULT OF THESE
STEPS. (BREATHE)

THIS EVENING I PRAY THAT BY MY EXAMPLE
TODAY OTHERS WHO STILL SUFFER
RECEIVED A MESSAGE OF HOPE. (BREATHE)

THIS EVENING I EXPRESS MY GRATITUDE
FOR THE ABILITY AND WILLINGNESS TO
PRACTICE THE PRINCIPLES OF THE STEPS IN
ALL ASPECTS OF MY LIFE.

(Finish with your ending ritual.)

Version Five
By What Name?

*"Men give different names to
one and the same thing from the
difference of their own passions."*

Thomas Hobbes (1588-1679)

"God Has Ninety-nine Names"

Book title by Judith Miller,

*"I bow to God, Who lives in this world
within us. Whoever calls Him by any
name, by that name does He come."*

William Buck

51

In version five you are asked to address your Higher Power by some name. A list of names is provided. I suggest that you try different names and pay attention to your reaction when you say each aloud. What does you reaction to these names tell you about your relationship to the Higher Power of your understanding? Does a certain name cause you to feel afraid, while another leads to comfort?

Names For The Spiritual Force In Your Recovery

Absolute	First Cause	Lord	Supreme Being
Adonai	First One	Lord of hosts	Tao
Ahura Mazda	Friend	Love	The All
All	G-d	Maker	The Beginner
Allah	God	Merciful One	The Boundless
Almighty One	Goddess	Mohammed	The Center
Beloved	Grandfather	Most High	The Light
Benevolent One	Grandmother	Mother Earth	The One
Brahma	Grandparent	Mysterious	The One
Buddha Nature	Great One	One	Above
Center	Great Spirit	Nature	The Source
Christ	Greater Self	One Heart	The Totality
Companion	Guide	One Source	That-Which-
Cosmic	Hashem	Oversoul	Imagined-Us
Intelligence	Heavenly	Parent	Ultimate
Creator	Father	Prince of peace	Source
Divine Entity	Higher Power	Protector	Universe
Divine Mind	Higher Self	Providence	Universal One
Divine Will	Holy Mystery	Redeemer	Vishnu
Dominus	Holy One	Sacred One	Wholeness
Earth Mother	Holy Spirit	Sat Guru	Wise One
Energy Of The	Inner Voice	Savior	Wiser Self
Universe	Jahweh	Shaddai	Yahweh
Essence Of	Jesus	Shepherd	You Who Are
Life	Kami	Soul	Called By Many
Essential One	King of Heaven	Source of	Names
Eternal Being	King of Kings	Being	
Eternal One	Krishna	Source of Life	
Father	Life Force	Son of God	

Version Five-Morning

(Start with your beginning ritual).

(Name) THIS MORNING I ADMIT WHEN I AM DISTANT FROM YOU I AM POWERLESS OVER (My affliction)-WHICH MAKES MY LIFE UNMANAGEABLE. (BREATHE)

(Name), THIS MORNING I BELIEVE THAT YOU ARE A POWER GREATER THAN MYSELF AND YOU CAN RESTORE ME TO SANITY. (BREATHE)

(Name), THIS MORNING I AM MAKING A DECISION TO TURN MY WILL AND MY LIFE OVER TO YOUR CARE. (BREATHE)

(Name), THIS MORNING I AM ENTIRELY READY TO HAVE YOU REMOVE ALL MY DEFECTS OF CHARACTER. (BREATHE)

(Name), THIS MORNING I HUMBLY ASK YOU TO REMOVE MY SHORTCOMINGS. (BREATHE)

(Name), THIS MORNING I SEEK THROUGH PRAYER AND MEDITATION TO IMPROVE MY CONSCIOUS CONTACT WITH YOU, PRAYING ONLY FOR KNOWLEDGE OF YOUR WILL FOR ME AND THE POWER TO CARRY THAT OUT. (BREATHE)

(Name), TODAY AS I EXPERIENCE A SPIRITUAL
AWAKENING AS A RESULT OF THESE STEPS,
I WILL TRY TO CARRY THE MESSAGE OF
RECOVERY TO OTHERS WHO STILL SUFFER
AND TO PRACTICE THE PRINCIPLES OF THE
STEPS IN ALL ASPECTS OF MY LIFE.

(Finish with your ending ritual.)

Version Five-Evening

(Start with your beginning ritual.)

(Name), TONIGHT I ADMIT WHEN DISTANT
FROM YOU I AM POWERLESS OVER (Affliction)-
THAT MY LIFE IS UNMANAGEABLE. (BREATHE)

(Name) TONIGHT I BELIEVE THAT YOU ARE
A POWER GREATER THAN MYSELF AND YOU
ARE RESTORING ME TO SANITY. (BREATHE)

(Name) TONIGHT I AM GRATEFUL THIS DAY
I WAS ABLE TO MAKE A DECISION TO TURN
MY WILL AND MY LIFE OVER TO YOUR CARE.
(BREATHE)

(Name) TONIGHT I CONTINUE TO BE
ENTIRELY WILLING TO HAVE YOU REMOVE
ALL MY DEFECTS OF CHARACTER. (BREATHE)

(Name) TONIGHT I HUMBLY ASK YOU TO
CONTINUE TO REMOVE MY SHORTCOMINGS.
(BREATHE)

(Name) TONIGHT I TAKE PERSONAL
INVENTORY AND FIND I HAVE BEEN WRONG
AND NOW PROMPTLY ADMIT IT. If after an honest review of the day you are unable to identify anyone you have harmed replace the above statement
with "after taking personal inventory I find I have

not harmed anyone," and skip the next two statements. (BREATHE)

(Name) TONIGHT I LIST THESE PERSONS I HAVE HARMED TODAY, AND AM WILLING TO MAKE AMENDS TO THEM ALL. (BREATHE)

(Name) TONIGHT I AGREE TO MAKE DIRECT AMENDS TO THESE PEOPLE WHEREVER POSSIBLE, EXCEPT WHEN TO DO SO WOULD INJURE THEM OR OTHERS. (BREATHE)

(Name) TONIGHT I AGAIN SEEK THROUGH PRAYER AND MEDITATION TO IMPROVE MY CONSCIOUS CONTACT WITH YOU, PRAYING ONLY FOR KNOWLEDGE OF YOUR WILL FOR ME AND THE POWER TO CARRY THAT OUT. (BREATHE)

(Name) TODAY I TRIED TO CARRY THIS MESSAGE TO OTHERS WHO STILL SUFFER AND PRACTICED THE PRINCIPLES OF THE STEPS IN ALL ASPECTS OF MY LIFE.

(Finish with your ending ritual.)

Conscious Contact

Version Six
My God...

To further personalize your relationship with your Higher Power in this version you are asked to try adding the word "My" to whatever name you are using for the Higher Power of your understanding. For example, rather than saying, "Protector, this morning I believe you are a power greater than myself," experience how you feel when you say "MY Protector..."

Version Six-Morning

(Start with your beginning ritual.)

MY (Name of Higher Power), THIS MORNING I ADMIT WHEN SPIRITUALLY ISOLATED I AM POWERLESS OVER (Affliction)-WHICH MAKES MY LIFE UNMANAGEABLE. (BREATHE)

MY (Name), THIS MORNING I BELIEVE THAT YOU ARE A POWER GREATER THAN MYSELF AND YOU CAN RESTORE ME TO SANITY. (BREATHE)

MY (Name), THIS MORNING I AM MAKING A DECISION TO TURN MY WILL AND MY LIFE OVER TO YOUR CARE. (BREATHE)

MY (Name), THIS MORNING I AM ENTIRELY READY TO HAVE YOU REMOVE ALL MY DEFECTS OF CHARACTER. (BREATHE)

MY (Name), THIS MORNING I HUMBLY ASK YOU TO REMOVE MY SHORTCOMINGS. (BREATHE)

MY (Name), THIS MORNING I SEEK THROUGH PRAYER AND MEDITATION TO IMPROVE MY CONSCIOUS CONTACT WITH YOU, PRAYING ONLY FOR KNOWLEDGE OF YOUR WILL FOR ME AND THE POWER TO CARRY THAT OUT. (BREATHE)

MY (Name), TODAY AS I EXPERIENCE A SPIRITUAL AWAKENING AS A RESULT OF THESE STEPS, I WILL TRY TO CARRY THIS MESSAGE TO OTHERS WHO STILL SUFFER AND TO PRACTICE THE PRINCIPLES OF RECOVERY IN ALL ASPECTS OF MY LIFE.

Version Six-Evening

(Start with your beginning ritual.)

MY (Name), TONIGHT I ADMIT WHEN SPIRITUALLY ISOLATED I AM POWERLESS OVER (Affliction)-THAT MY LIFE IS UNMANAGEABLE. (BREATHE)

MY (Name), TONIGHT I TURN MY WILL AND MY LIFE OVER TO YOUR CARE. (BREATHE)

MY (Name), TONIGHT I CONTINUE TO BE ENTIRELY WILLING TO HAVE YOU REMOVE ALL MY DEFECTS OF CHARACTER. (BREATHE)

MY (Name), TONIGHT I HUMBLY ASK YOU TO CONTINUE TO REMOVE MY SHORTCOMINGS. (BREATHE)

MY (Name), TONIGHT I TAKE PERSONAL INVENTORY AND FIND I HAVE BEEN WRONG AND NOW PROMPTLY ADMIT IT. If after an honest review of the day you are unable to identify anyone you have harmed skip the next two statements. (BREATHE)

MY (Name), TONIGHT I LIST THESE PERSONS I HAVE HARMED TODAY, AND AM WILLING TO MAKE AMENDS TO THEM ALL. (BREATHE)

MY (Name), TONIGHT I AGREE TO MAKE DIRECT AMENDS TO THESE PEOPLE WHEREVER POSSIBLE, EXCEPT WHEN TO DO SO WOULD INJURE THEM OR OTHERS. (BREATHE)

MY (Name), TONIGHT I AGAIN SEEK THROUGH PRAYER AND MEDITATION TO IMPROVE MY CONSCIOUS CONTACT WITH YOU, PRAYING ONLY FOR KNOWLEDGE OF YOUR WILL FOR ME AND THE POWER TO CARRY THAT OUT. (BREATHE)

MY (Name), TODAY I TRIED TO CARRY THIS MESSAGE TO OTHERS WHO STILL SUFFER AND TO PRACTICE THE PRINCIPLES OF RECOVERY IN ALL ASPECTS OF MY LIFE.

(Finish with your ending ritual.)

Version Seven
Improvisation On A Theme

As you probably have noticed with each version the prayers become more complex. As with anything worth doing prayer is most powerful when practiced, and with practice comes an increase in confidence and skill. By the time you are utilizing this seventh version you will have become comfortable with the format, and are ready to enhance the prayer with more of your personal experience. I have included examples to illustrate how one can customize this version with personal details. Once you have practiced the various versions you can improvise your own versions by utilizing aspects of them. This will help keep your prayer vibrant and meaningful.

Version Seven- Morning

MY HIGHER POWER, THIS MORNING I ADMIT
WHEN I AM ISOLATED FROM OTHERS IN
RECOVERY I AM POWERLESS OVER MY
ADDICTION-THAT WITHOUT SOBRIETY MY
LIFE IS UNMANAGEABLE. WHEN NOT SOBER I
FIND MYSELF ACTING IN WAYS THAT VIOLATE
MY VALUES, SUCH AS LYING, AND VIOLATING
MY MARRIAGE VOWS.

MY HIGHER POWER, THIS MORNING
I BELIEVE THAT YOU ARE A POWER
GREATER THAN MYSELF AND YOU CAN,
AND WILL, RESTORE ME TO SANITY. BEING
RESTORED TO SANITY MEANS I WILL BE
FREE OF ADDICTIVE BEHAVIORS AND SELF-
DESTRUCTIVE URGES.

HOLY ONE, THIS MORNING I AM MAKING A
DECISION TO TURN MY WILL AND MY LIFE
OVER TO YOUR CARE. I WILL DEMONSTRATE
THIS DECISION BY ATTENDING A TWELVE
STEP MEETING. I WILL LISTEN TO WHAT IS
BEING SAID WITH AN OPEN MIND AND APPLY
WHAT I HEAR FROM OTHERS TO MY LIFE.
I WILL AVOID PLACES AND PEOPLE THAT
TRIGGER ADDICTIVE URGES.

WISE SELF, THIS MORNING I AM ENTIRELY
READY TO HAVE YOU REMOVE ALL MY

DEFECTS OF CHARACTER, THOSE OF WHICH I
AM AWARE AND THOSE TO WHICH I AM STILL
BLIND.

SPIRIT, THIS MORNING I HUMBLY ASK YOU TO
REMOVE MY SHORTCOMINGS. IN PARTICULAR
I ASK THAT YOU REMOVE MY HABIT OF
BEING JUDGMENTAL, AND REPLACE IT WITH
ACCEPTANCE AND TOLERANCE OF OTHERS.
I ASK THAT YOU REMOVE MY MATERIALISM,
AND REPLACE IT WITH GRATITUDE AND
CONTENTMENT.

MY GENTLE GUIDE, THIS MORNING I SEEK
THROUGH PRAYER AND MEDITATION TO
IMPROVE MY CONSCIOUS CONTACT WITH
YOU, PRAYING ONLY FOR KNOWLEDGE OF
YOUR WILL FOR ME AND THE POWER TO
CARRY THAT OUT. I WILL KNOW WHEN I AM
CARRYING OUT YOUR WILL WHEN I CAN
ENGAGE IN A BEHAVIOR WITHOUT KEEPING
IT SECRET.

GOD, TODAY AS I EXPERIENCE A SPIRITUAL
AWAKENING AS A RESULT OF THESE STEPS,
I WILL TRY TO CARRY THIS MESSAGE TO
OTHERS WHO STILL SUFFER AND TO
PRACTICE THESE PRINCIPLES IN ALL I DO.
TODAY I WILL CALL AT LEAST ONE MEMBER
OF MY GROUP AND OFFER MY EXPERIENCE,
STRENGTH, AND HOPE.

Conscious Contact

Version Seven- Evening

CREATOR, TONIGHT I ADMIT WITHOUT THE
ASSISTANCE OF YOU AND OTHER PEOPLE
I AM POWERLESS, AND THAT WITHOUT
RECOVERY MY LIFE IS UNMANAGEABLE. I AM
GRATEFUL THAT TODAY I AM A *RECOVERING*
ADDICT.

MY CREATOR, TONIGHT I BELIEVE THAT
YOU ARE A POWER GREATER THAN MYSELF
AND TODAY YOU RESTORED ME TO SANITY.
I KNOW THIS BECAUSE ALL THIS DAY I
WAS FREE OF COMPULSIVE ACTS AND
SELF-DESTRUCTIVE THOUGHTS. WHEN I
WAS STRESSED I TURNED TO YOU AND TO
OTHERS RATHER THAN RUNNING TO MY
ADDICTION.

SOURCE OF LIFE, TONIGHT I AM GRATEFUL
THIS DAY I WAS ABLE TO MAKE A DECISION
TO TURN MY WILL AND MY LIFE OVER TO
YOUR CARE. I AM GRATEFUL THAT I KNOW OF
THE TWELVE STEP PROGRAM, AND LIVE IN A
PLACE WHERE I HAVE ACCESS TO MEETINGS.
THANK YOU FOR THE MANY WAYS I WAS
CARED FOR TODAY.

GREAT SPIRIT, TONIGHT I CONTINUE TO BE
ENTIRELY WILLING TO HAVE YOU REMOVE
ALL MY DEFECTS OF CHARACTER. I AM AWARE

THAT TODAY MY DEFECT OF MATERIALISM
WAS REMOVED. WHEN STRESSED I MADE A
PHONE CALL TO MY SPONSOR RATHER THAN
GOING SHOPPING OR FANTASIZING ABOUT
BUYING THINGS AND THINKING THAT
WOULD MAKE ME HAPPY.

MY PROTECTOR, TONIGHT I HUMBLY
ASK YOU TO CONTINUE TO REMOVE MY
SHORTCOMINGS. EVEN AS I SLEEP, HEAL MY
MIND FROM MY ADDICTIVE THINKING AND
DEPRESSED MOOD.

SPIRIT OF FORGIVENESS, TONIGHT I TAKE
PERSONAL INVENTORY AND FIND I HAVE
BEEN WRONG, AND NOW PROMPTLY ADMIT
IT TO YOU. MY GUILT ALLOWS ME TO KNOW
WHEN I HAVE WRONGED ANOTHER.

SPIRIT OF GOODNESS, TONIGHT I ADMIT I
HARMED A FELLOW GROUP MEMBER TODAY
BY ENGAGING IN GOSSIP ABOUT HIM WITH A
THIRD GROUP MEMBER, AND I AM WILLING
TO MAKE AMENDS TO HIM.

MY GUIDE, TONIGHT SINCE I SINCERELY
BELIEVE IT WOULD NOT INJURE HIM OR
OTHERS, I AGREE TO MAKE DIRECT AMENDS
TO THIS PERSON, BY APOLOGIZING TO HIM
TOMORROW WITHOUT MENTIONING THE
OTHER GROUP MEMBER'S NAME. I WILL
FURTHER MAKE AMENDS BY NOT ENGAGING

IN GOSSIP IN THE FUTURE. I WILL CALL THE
THIRD PERSON INVOLVED AND TELL HIM I
WAS WRONG TO ENGAGE IN GOSSIP.

MY GUIDE, TONIGHT I AGAIN SEEK THROUGH
THIS PRAYER AND MEDITATION TO IMPROVE
MY CONSCIOUS CONTACT WITH YOU,
PRAYING ONLY FOR KNOWLEDGE OF YOUR
WILL FOR ME AND THE POWER TO CARRY
THAT OUT. I BELIEVE IT IS YOUR WILL FOR
ME THAT I REMAIN SOBER AND PRACTICING
THE PRINCIPLES OF THE TWELVE STEPS.

LOVING FORCE, TODAY I EXPERIENCED A
SPIRITUAL AWAKENING AS A RESULT OF
WORKING THE TWELVE STEPS. I WAS FREE OF
ADDICTIVE URGES AND SELF-DESTRUCTIVE
THOUGHTS.

UNIVERSAL SPIRIT, TODAY I TRIED TO CARRY
THIS MESSAGE TO OTHERS WHO STILL
SUFFER BY ATTENDING A MEETING AND
EXPRESSING MY GRATITUDE FOR RECOVERY.

HIGHER POWER, TODAY I PRACTICED THE
PRINCIPLES OF RECOVERY IN ALL I DID. IN
MY BUSINESS I TREATED ALL MY CUSTOMERS
AND CO-WORKERS WITH RESPECT,
GENEROSITY, AND KINDNESS. I WAS ABLE TO
DO THIS THANKS TO THE SELF-ACCEPTANCE
I HAVE DEVELOPED FROM WORKING THE
STEPS.

MY GENTLE LORD, TODAY (OTHER THAN THE HARM I CAUSED TO MY FELLOW GROUP MEMBER) I DID NOTHING THAT I WOULD BE EMBARRASSED TO DO IN FRONT OF YOU, MY SPONSOR OR MY SPOUSE.

Version Seven 2.0- Morning

(Start with beginning ritual.)

MY (Name), THIS MORNING I ADMIT
WHEN ISOLATED I AM POWERLESS OVER
(Affliction). AS A RESULT OF MY AFFLICTION
MY LIFE TODAY IS UNMANAGEABLE IN THE
FOLLOWING WAYS (List). (BREATHE)

MY (Name), THIS MORNING I BELIEVE THAT
YOU ARE A POWER GREATER THAN MYSELF
AND YOU CAN RESTORE ME TO SANITY. FOR
ME BEING RESTORED TO SANITY INCLUDES
(Describe). (BREATHE)

MY (Name), THIS MORNING I AM MAKING A
DECISION TO TURN MY WILL AND MY LIFE
OVER TO YOUR CARE. I WILL DEMONSTRATE
THIS DECISION BY (Describe). (BREATHE)

MY (Name), THIS MORNING I AM ENTIRELY
READY TO HAVE YOU REMOVE ALL MY
DEFECTS OF CHARACTER. List one or two on
which you will focus today. (BREATHE)

MY (Name), THIS MORNING I HUMBLY ASK
YOU TO REMOVE MY SHORTCOMINGS. List one
or two character traits you would like to develop to
replace the defects you listed above. (BREATHE)

MY (Name), THIS MORNING WITH
WILLINGNESS, HONESTLY, AND AN OPEN
MIND I SEEK THROUGH THIS PRAYER AND
MEDITATION TO IMPROVE MY CONSCIOUS
CONTACT WITH YOU, PRAYING ONLY FOR
KNOWLEDGE OF YOUR WILL FOR ME AND
THE POWER TO CARRY THAT OUT. Wait and lis-
ten for guidance. (BREATHE)

MY (Name), TODAY AS I EXPERIENCE A
SPIRITUAL AWAKENING AS A RESULT OF
THESE STEPS, I WILL TRY TO CARRY THIS
MESSAGE TO OTHERS WHO STILL SUFFER
AND TO PRACTICE THESE PRINCIPLES IN ALL
MY ACTIONS. Describe what you will do and not
do.

(Finish with your ending ritual.)

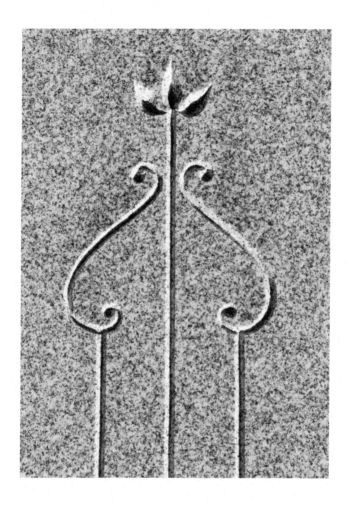

Version Seven 2.0- Evening

(Start with your beginning ritual.)

MY (Name), TONIGHT I ADMIT WITH MY WILL ALONE I AM POWERLESS OVER (Affliction) WHICH PUTS ME AT RISK FOR AN UNMANAGEABLE LIFE. (BREATHE)

MY (Name), TONIGHT I BELIEVE THAT YOU ARE A POWER GREATER THAN MYSELF, AND YOU ARE RESTORING ME TO SANITY. Describe how that fact is evident to you tonight. (BREATHE)

MY (Name), TONIGHT I AM GRATEFUL THIS DAY I WAS ABLE TO MAKE A DECISION TO TURN MY WILL AND MY LIFE OVER TO YOUR CARE. Describe how your life was made easier this day by your decision to rely on a spiritual program rather than your will alone. (BREATHE)

MY (Name), TONIGHT I AM AWARE OF YOU REMOVING MY DEFECTS OF CHARACTER. Describe how the defects on which you focused this morning and/or others were reduced or eliminated. (BREATHE)

MY (Name), TONIGHT I HUMBLY ASK YOU TO CONTINUE TO REMOVE MY SHORTCOMINGS. (BREATHE)

MY (Name), TONIGHT I TAKE PERSONAL INVENTORY AND FIND I HAVE BEEN WRONG AND NOW PROMPTLY ADMIT IT TO YOU. If after an honest review of the day you are unable to identify anyone you have harmed skip the next two statements. (BREATHE)

MY (Name), TONIGHT I LIST THESE PERSONS I HAVE HARMED TODAY, AND AM WILLING TO MAKE AMENDS TO THEM ALL. (BREATHE)

MY (Name), TONIGHT I AGREE TO MAKE DIRECT AMENDS TO THESE PEOPLE WHEREVER POSSIBLE, EXCEPT WHEN TO DO SO WOULD INJURE THEM OR OTHERS. Describe how you will do this, and when. (BREATHE)

MY (Name), TONIGHT I AGAIN SEEK THROUGH MY PRAYER AND MEDITATION TO IMPROVE MY CONSCIOUS CONTACT WITH YOU, PRAYING ONLY FOR KNOWLEDGE OF YOUR WILL FOR ME AND THE POWER TO CARRY THAT OUT. Wait, listen, and state what you believe God's will for you to be. (BREATHE)

MY (Name), TODAY I EXPERIENCED A SPIRITUAL AWAKENING AS A RESULT OF THESE STEPS. Describe. (BREATHE)

MY (Name), TODAY I TRIED TO CARRY THIS
MESSAGE TO OTHERS WHO STILL SUFFER.
Describe. (BREATHE)

MY (Name), TODAY I PRACTICED THESE
PRINCIPLES BY _____. Describe what you
did or didn't do that shows your life being consistent with the teachings of the Steps and Traditions.
If you did not practice these principles in all your
affairs, then return to the sections above where you
list the person(s) you harmed, and how you will
make amends.)

(Finish with your ending ritual.)

Version Eight
In Time Of Relapse

"**relapse**, to slip or slide back; to return; to slip or fall back into a former condition, especially after improvement or seeming improvement; specifically to fall back into illness after recovery or seeming recovery; to fall back into bad habits, wrongdoing, error, etc."

Webster's Dictionary

It is sometimes said that the term slip is an acronym for Something Lacking In Program. That *something* is often a lack of spirituality or conscious contact with a Higher Power. The problem may be a lack of belief, but it must be stressed that merely having a belief in a higher power isn't enough; an on-going relationship with that Higher Power is required. Even a strong belief in the effectiveness of even the most powerful medication is worthless if the medication isn't ingested. So, too, it is with spirituality; if one does not practice spiritual principles, a spiritual awakening will not take place, regardless of the strength of one's beliefs.

"Prior to my slip I thought I had finally hit bottom, but I must have bounced, 'cause here I am hitting bottom again."

Frank G., S.A.A. member

When does relapse begin? For those who take their affliction seriously the answer is, "The moment I forget that this affliction can rapidly lead to insane thinking and behavior, and death." Of course the next question is, "When does a relapse end?" For those who diligently practice the Twelve Steps the answer to that question is, "The moment I actively begin to work the Steps, particularly the first three Steps."

After a slip people often exclaim, "Now I am back to square one. I have to start all over again." Taking this viewpoint makes as much sense to me as a man walking across the ice on a frozen lake who slips and falls down, getting up and heading all the way back to where he first came from and retracing his path. What makes more sense is for him to stand up where he fell and continue to advance being more careful how he walks. In recovery when a person who had been abstinent for six weeks slips, the six weeks of growth he had gained were not eliminated by the relapse. Rather than describing a slip as a <u>loss</u> of abstinence it might be more accurate to describe it as an <u>interruption</u> of abstinence.

Every relapse ought to be taken seriously, since it can lead to arrest, death, or other consequences, but it must also be noted that some people gain very important information from a slip. Theologian Thomas Moore put it this way, "We may need to back step and regress. Growth, so often these days assumed automatically to be a goal in psychology and in life in general, can become a sentimental value that overlooks the necessity of such things as stagnancy and slippage...We are who we are as much because of our gaps and failures as because of our strengths."[20]

I have always thought there ought to be a word to describe a relapse that leads to improved recovery. A word that indicates something valuable has been learned that makes future relapse less likely. However, far too many people don't learn from their relapse; either they don't take the slip seriously and continue on as they had before, changing nothing, somehow expecting that another relapse won't happen, or they take it far too seriously and are so hard on themselves for having relapsed that their guilt and shame drives them into a binge.

In this section in addition to a Twelve Step-based prayer, I have included a prayer by Reverend Jeffery Sartain that addresses the struggle many people have when it comes to admitting relapse and disclosing it.

God Here Is What We Want To Be

God, here is what we want to be: independent, self-sufficient, strong, and self-assured. God, here is what we strive to convey: confidence, cheerfulness, valor, and determination. God, here is what we hope to offer: charity, generosity, sympathy, and tolerance. God, what we want to be, to convey, and to offer arises from strength.

But you know, as we know, we are not always strong. Here is how we feel so often: fragile, weak, wounded, and unsure. Here is how we try to cover it up: defensiveness, judgmentalism, and a façade of assurance. Denying our pain, disguising our weakness, veiling our fear, here is what we often offer: a shallow hope, an empty consolation, or unwanted advice.

But you know, as we know God, there is much to offer from our weakness, if we might only appreciate its treasures. The heart splayed wide open offers true compassion because it is acquainted with grief. The soul with fresh wounds and honest suffering brings comfort because that one acknowledges what is real and true. The arms tired and bruised can no longer embrace, but they can be embraced. Even in their fragile condition they sustain life-for what is life without the opportunity to carry the wounded? How can compassion find expression if no one reveals the marks of their injuries? How might you, our God, be real to us if it were not for vulnerability, humility, even pain and grief?

It cannot be explained, but we know what is true. We are stronger when our strength is built on the foundation of our honest pain. We are more compassionate when our caring for others arises from our most vulnerable wounds. We are only truly self-sufficient and assured when we know how to ask for help and receive it graciously and thankfully.

These are mysteries of human community and mysteries of faith.[21]

Version Eight-Morning

"The heart's cry to God is the highest form of prayer."

Zohar, 13th century Jewish mystic

(Start with your beginning ritual.)

THIS MORNING I ADMIT I AM POWERLESS
OVER (Affliction) WHICH IS MAKING MY
LIFE UNMANAGEABLE. I AM CURRENTLY
SUFFERING FROM RELAPSE.

THIS MORNING I BELIEVE THAT YOU ARE A
POWER GREATER THAN MYSELF AND YOU
CAN RESTORE ME TO SANITY, WHICH MEANS
I DO NOT HAVE TO COPE WITH THESE
RELAPSE SYMPTOMS ALONE BECAUSE HELP IS
AVAILABLE TO ME.

THIS MORNING I AM MAKING A DECISION
TO TURN MY WILL AND MY LIFE OVER TO
YOUR CARE. I WILL ACCEPT THE HELP THAT
IS AVAILABLE TO ME. I WILL DO THIS BY
_____. Describe what actions you will take,
e.g. attending a meeting, calling your sponsor, etc.

THIS MORNING I AM ENTIRELY READY
TO HAVE YOU REMOVE ALL MY DEFECTS
OF CHARACTER. I AM READY TO BE FREE
OF RELAPSE AND THOSE DEFECTS OF

CHARACTER THAT CONTRIBUTED TO IT. List one or two defects. e.g. thinking you could do it alone, believing you are different, worse or better, than others with your affliction, rationalizing your situation is unique, etc.

THIS MORNING I HUMBLY ASK YOU TO REMOVE MY SHORTCOMINGS. IN PARTICULAR I ASK THAT MY (Affliction) BE REMOVED.

THIS MORNING I SEEK THROUGH PRAYER AND MEDITATION TO IMPROVE MY CONSCIOUS CONTACT WITH YOU, PRAYING ONLY FOR KNOWLEDGE OF YOUR WILL FOR ME AND THE POWER TO CARRY THAT OUT. I BELIEVE IT IS YOUR WILL FOR ME THAT I BE RELIEVED OF MY (Affliction).

TODAY AS I SEEK TO EXPERIENCE A SPIRITUAL AWAKENING AS A RESULT OF THESE STEPS, I WILL ALLOW OTHERS TO CARRY YOUR MESSAGE TO ME BECAUSE I AM STILL SUFFERING. I WILL ONCE AGAIN BEGIN TO PRACTICE THE PRINCIPLES OF RECOVERY IN ALL ASPECTS OF MY LIFE (Describe).

(Finish with your ending ritual.)

Version Eight-Evening

(Start with your beginning ritual.)

TONIGHT ONCE AGAIN I ADMIT MY POWERLESS OVER MY AFFLICTION-THAT MY LIFE CAN EASILY BECOME UNMANAGEABLE.

TONIGHT I BELIEVE THAT YOU ARE A POWER GREATER THAN MYSELF AND YOU ARE RESTORING ME TO SANITY. I BELIEVE THIS BECAUSE TODAY I WAS RELIEVED OF THE BEHAVIORS ASSOCIATED WITH MY AFFLICTION.

TONIGHT I AM GRATEFUL THIS DAY I WAS ABLE TO MAKE A DECISION TO TURN MY WILL AND MY LIFE OVER TO YOUR CARE. I REMIND MYSELF OF THE WAYS I DID THIS (Describe).

TONIGHT I CONTINUE TO BE ENTIRELY WILLING TO HAVE YOU REMOVE ALL MY DEFECTS OF CHARACTER. I CONTINUE TO BE WILLING TO BE FREE OF THE THOUGHTS AND BEHAVIORS ASSOCIATED WITH MY AFFLICTION.

TONIGHT I HUMBLY ASK YOU TO CONTINUE TO REMOVE MY SHORTCOMINGS. IN ADDITION TO MY AFFLICTION I ASK THAT

YOU REMOVE THOSE SHORTCOMINGS THAT CONTRIBUTED TO MY RELAPSE (List these).

TONIGHT I TAKE PERSONAL INVENTORY AND FIND I HAVE BEEN WRONG AND NOW PROMPTLY ADMIT IT. (If after an honest review of the day you are unable to identify anyone you have harmed, skip the next two statements.)

TONIGHT I LIST THESE PERSONS I HAVE HARMED TODAY, AND AM WILLING TO MAKE AMENDS TO THEM ALL.

TONIGHT I AGREE TO MAKE DIRECT AMENDS TO THESE PEOPLE WHEREVER POSSIBLE, EXCEPT WHEN TO DO SO WOULD INJURE THEM OR OTHERS. (Describe how and when you will make direct or indirect amends.)

TONIGHT I AGAIN SEEK THROUGH PRAYER AND MEDITATION TO IMPROVE MY CONSCIOUS CONTACT WITH YOU, PRAYING ONLY FOR KNOWLEDGE OF YOUR WILL FOR ME AND THE POWER TO CARRY THAT OUT. I BELIEVE IT IS YOUR WILL FOR ME THAT I EXPERIENCE A REPRIEVE FROM MY AFFLICTION.

TODAY I EXPERIENCED A SPIRITUAL AWAKENING AS A RESULT OF THE STEPS, BY BEING ABLE TO REMAIN SOBER.

TODAY I LET OTHERS CARRY THE MESSAGE
OF RECOVERY TO ME. (Describe how you did
this.)

TODAY I PRACTICED THE PRINCIPLES OF
RECOVERY TO THE BEST OF MY ABILITIES.
(Describe the things you did and didn't do that
were consistent with the Steps.)

(Finish with your ending ritual.)

Conscious Contact

Version Eight-Evening -

When Relapse Has Continued

" 'And this too, shall pass away.' How much it expresses. How consoling in the depths of affliction. 'And this too, shall pass away.' "

Abraham Lincoln

(Start with your beginning ritual.)

TONIGHT I ADMIT MY POWERLESS OVER (Affliction)-THAT MY LIFE CONTINUES TO BE UNMANAGEABLE (Describe how you are suffering as a result of your powerlessness and its negative effects in all areas of your life).

TONIGHT I BELIEVE THAT YOU ARE A POWER GREATER THAN MYSELF AND YOU ARE ABLE TO RESTORE ME TO SANITY. I BELIEVE I WILL NOT RECEIVE A DAILY REPRIEVE FROM MY AFFLICTION AS LONG AS I NEGLECT MY SPIRITUAL CONDITION.

TONIGHT I AM MAKING A DECISION TO TURN MY WILL AND MY LIFE OVER TO YOUR CARE. I WANT TO BELIEVE I AM WORTHY OF YOUR CARE.

TONIGHT I AM BECOMING WILLING TO
HAVE YOU REMOVE ALL MY DEFECTS OF
CHARACTER. IN PARTICULAR I AM ENTIRELY
READY TO HAVE MY URGE TO ENGAGE IN MY
AFFLICTION REMOVED.

TONIGHT I HUMBLY ASK YOU TO REMOVE MY
SHORTCOMINGS THAT CONTRIBUTE TO ME
ENGAGING IN MY AFFLICTION. I AM AWARE
OF THE FOLLOWING SHORTCOMINGS IN
WHICH I AM ACTIVELY ENGAGING (List).

TONIGHT I TAKE PERSONAL INVENTORY
AND FIND I HAVE BEEN WRONG AND NOW
PROMPTLY ADMIT IT. (List the ways you did
wrong that contributed to continued relapse or
other problem behavior.)

TONIGHT I LIST THESE PERSONS I HAVE
HARMED TODAY, AND AM WILLING TO MAKE
AMENDS TO THEM ALL. I INCLUDE MYSELF
ON THIS LIST SINCE I HARMED MYSELF BY
TAKING PART IN MY AFFLICTION.

TONIGHT I AGREE TO MAKE DIRECT AMENDS
TO THE PEOPLE I HARMED WHEREVER
POSSIBLE, EXCEPT WHEN TO DO SO WOULD
INJURE THEM OR OTHERS (Describe when and
how). I WILL MAKE AMENDS TO MYSELF BY
ACCEPTING YOUR HELP AND THE HELP OF
OTHER PEOPLE SO THAT I MAY RECOVER
MY SANITY AND STOP ENGAGING IN MY

AFFLICTION.

TONIGHT WITH WILLINGNESS, HONESTY,
AND AN OPEN MIND, I SEEK THROUGH THIS
PRAYER AND MEDITATION TO IMPROVE MY
CONSCIOUS CONTACT WITH YOU, PRAYING
ONLY FOR KNOWLEDGE OF YOUR WILL FOR
ME AND THE POWER TO CARRY THAT OUT.
I BELIEVE IT IS YOUR WILL THAT I OBTAIN
AND MAINTAIN ABSTINENCE FROM SELF-
DESTRUCTIVE BEHAVIORS.

TODAY I BELIEVE I CAN OBTAIN A SPIRITUAL
AWAKENING IF I AM WILLING TO PRACTICE
THESE STEPS AND PRINCIPLES IN ALL
ASPECTS OF MY LIFE.

(Finish with your ending ritual.)

Prayer Within Meetings

In many Twelve Step groups part of the ritual used to begin the meeting is a moment of silence or meditation following a brief reading. I have often heard people complain they are uncomfortable during this time because they are not sure on what to focus their attention. In order to address this concern I am providing a number of brief prayers based on the Steps that can be utilized at these times.

A Prayer Based On The Second And Third Steps
I BELIEVE THESE PEOPLE ARE A POWER
GREATER THAN MYSELF ALONE, AND
THEY CAN HELP RESTORE ME TO SANITY.
THEREFORE, DURING THIS MEETING I AM
TURNING MY WILL AND LIFE OVER TO THEIR
CARE. I WILL DO THIS BY LISTENING TO
THEM WITH AN OPEN MIND, AND SPEAKING
WITH AN OPEN HEART.

A Prayer Based On The Fourth And Fifth Steps
DURING THIS MEETING I WILL MAKE
AN INVENTORY OF MYSELF SO THAT I CAN
ADMIT TO YOU, MYSELF, AND TO THE
OTHERS GATHERED HERE, MY CURRENT
MORAL CONDITION.

A Prayer Based On The Sixth And Seventh Steps
I AM ENTIRELY READY TO HAVE ALL MY
IMPERFECTIONS REMOVED SO THAT I CAN

BE HUMBLE ENOUGH TO LEARN FROM THE OTHERS GATHERED HERE IN THE SPIRIT OF RECOVERY.

A Prayer Based On The Eleventh Step

I PRAY DURING THIS MEETING I WILL HAVE CONSCIOUS CONTACT WITH YOU, MY HIGHER POWER, AND WITH THESE OTHER PEOPLE, SO I CAN OBTAIN KNOWLEDGE OF WHAT IS RIGHT AND GOOD, METHODS TO CARRY THAT OUT, AND THE WILLINGNESS TO TAKE THE NECESSARY ACTIONS.

A Prayer Based On The Twelfth Step

DURING THIS MEETING I PRAY FOR SPIRITUAL AWAKENING SO THAT I MAY CARRY THE MESSAGE OF RECOVERY TO OTHERS WHO ARE NOW IN THIS ROOM WITH ME.

Prayer Based On Multiple Steps

(GOD), I ADMIT WHEN ISOLATED I AM POWERLESS OVER (Affliction)-WHICH CAN MAKE MY LIFE UNMANAGEABLE. I BELIEVE THAT YOU, AND THESE PEOPLE GATHERED TOGETHER, ARE A POWER GREATER THAN MYSELF ALONE. THEREFORE, I GRATEFULLY TURN MY WILL AND LIFE OVER TO BE CARED FOR. DURING THIS MEETING I WILL BE FEARLESS IN MY PERSONAL SEARCHING. I WILL HONESTLY ADMIT TO YOU, MYSELF, AND TO THESE OTHERS, MY EXACT MORAL CONDITION. I WILL ADMIT WHEN I AM

WRONG. I WILL BE OPEN TO LEARNING THAT
I HAVE HARMED OTHERS. I WILL BE ENTIRELY
READY TO HAVE ANY AND ALL DEFECTS
REMOVED SO I CAN HAVE CONSCIOUS
CONTACT WITH YOU AND THE GROUP
MEMBERS. MAY MY PRESENCE HERE IN THIS
PLACE SERVE TO CARRY THE MESSAGE OF
RECOVERY TO OTHERS, AND TO CONTINUE
TO ADVANCE MY SPIRITUAL AWAKENING.

Bibliography

A.A. (1953). *Twelve Steps And Twelve Traditions* , A. A. World Services, NY, NY.

A.A. (1976). *Alcoholics Anonymous* , A. A. World Services, NY, NY.

E. L. (2010). A Seventh Step Prayer. *The Outer Circle*, vol. 4 (4), July-Aug. p. 32.

Hunter, M. (1988,). *The Twelve Steps & Shame*, Center City, MN: Hazelden Educational Materials.

Jackson, E.N. (1968). *Understanding Prayer.* New York, NY: Harper and Row.

Moore, T. (1992). *Care Of The Soul.* New York, NY: Harper Perennial.

Reber, A. S. (1985). *Dictionary Of Psychology.* New York, NY: Penguin Books.

Sheldrake, R. (2002). *The Sense Of Being Stared At.* New York, NY: Crown Publishers.

Woodruff, P. (2001). *Reverence: Renewing A Forgotten Virtue.* New York, NY: Oxford Press.

About The Author

Dr. Mic Hunter is best known as the author of *Abused Boys: The Neglected Victims Of Sexual Abuse.* He is licensed as both a psychologist and as a marriage and family therapist. He first began working with recovering people in 1978, and has spoken and written extensively on the Twelve Steps. In 1999 The National Organization on Male Sexual Victimization awarded him their highest honor, *The Fay Honey Knopp Memorial Award,* "For recognition of his contributions to the field of male sexual victimization treatment and knowledge." In 2007 the Board of Directors of Male Survivor created *The Mic Hunter Award For Research Advances.* As its first recipient Dr. Hunter was cited for his, "Ceaseless pursuit of knowledge about male sexual abuse in all its occurrences, of the eloquent dissemination of new knowledge in this area, and of the stimulation for further study and concern about revealing, treating and preventing male sexual abuse." He is the author of numerous books including, *Back To The Source: The Spirituality Of Jesus,* that focuses on the overlap of the teachings of Jesus and the principles of the Twelve Steps. Since 2000 he has facilitated a couples communication retreat on the campus of the renowned Hazelden treatment center. He has given presentations to professional audiences and the general public hundreds of times both in America and other countries. He is frequently called upon by the print and broadcast media to speak on psychological issues, including *Oprah, CNN,* and *The Wall Street Journal.*

About The Photographs

All the photographs used in this book were created by Mic Hunter during his travels and are details of tombstones. They are a sub-group from a larger photography project on cemeteries.

End Notes

1   A.A., 1976, page 53.
2   A.A., 1976, page 44.
3   A.A., 1976, page 85.
4   A.A 1953; Hunter, 1988,
5   Reber, 1985.
6   Moore, 1992, p. 211
7   Moore, 1992, p. 211
8   Moore, 1992, p. 225
9   A. A., 1953
10   Sheldrake, 2002.
11   Moore, 1992, p. 227.
12   *Mark* 2:27.
13   Jackson, 1968, pp. 5-6.
14   Jackson, 1968, p. 29.
15   Woodruff, 2001, p. 19.
16   Larry E., 2010.
17   A.A., 1976, page 60.
18   A.A., 1976, p. 569.
19   A.A., 1976, pp. 63 & 76.
20   Moore, 1992, pp 50 & 51.
21   Reverend Jeffery Sartain, Pastoral prayer 2/1/04, Plymouth Congregational Church, Minneapolis, Minnesota, used with permission.

CPSIA information can be obtained
at www.ICGtesting.com
Printed in the USA
LVOW04s1355181215
467171LV00022B/481/P